WORK FR(

PRODUCTIVE HACKS

HOW TO STAY MOTIVATED WORKING FROM YOUR COMFORT ZONE DURING AND AFTER THE CORONA VIRUS

DANIEL WELSH

Daniel Welsh

©COPYRIGHT

Daniel Welsh

TABLE OF CONTENT

DEDICATION

I am dedicating this book to my wonderful family and to you
reading it right now

INTRODUCTION

T This ain't another post about Pomodoro, time-blocking, finding your "optimal work time", or any other of those other common work from home productivity tips you've heard 1000 times.

That's all good stuff. But if it was working, would you be reading this?

No. It's time to think outside the box.

The outbreak of the coronavirus has more people working from home than ever. Much of the world is on the second wave of the lockdown to curb the spread, and, even in places that aren't, people are encouraged to stay at home.

Where it's possible, employers are encouraging or requiring people to work from home for an indeterminate amount of time.

So if you're one of the newcomers in the work-from-home lifestyle, whether due to the pandemic or because you've managed to secure a remote-based job, you'll need to change some of your habits and routines to make working from home a success.

There are plenty of benefits of working from home, from being able to see more of your family to a flexible schedule and more. No wonder people are all moving into the freelancing community en masse.

On the flip side, working from home is very dangerous if you're easily lured in by procrastination or easily swayed by the numerous distractions that can present themselves and hamper your productivity.

Naturally, we all face various challenges in life not only because of our different personalities but also due to our various lifestyles and the type of work we do. Still, many of the core issues we face as remote employees are the same.

Everyone who works remotely has to figure out when to work, where to work, and how to create boundaries between work and personal life.

In this guide, I will show you some new and creative work-from-home productivity hacks you've probably never thought of before.

CHAPTER 1

NON-CONVENTIONAL METHODS OF WORK FROM HOME PRODUCTIVITY HACKS

Wait till the very last minute

Whoever claims procrastination doesn't boost productivity has obviously never finished a 20-page research paper the night before it's due. Work expands to fit the time available to complete it.

In 1970, a magazine, not very popular then, hired a young journalist to cover the Kentucky Derby. The journalist attended the race and took notes, but when it came to actually writing the piece, he was seriously delayed.

When the deadline came, in lieu of a completed article, he hastily ripped out pages from his notebook and sent them off to the press.

While that severe procrastination and haphazard work could easily have been the end of his career, the result proved otherwise.

The resulting article, "The Kentucky Derby Is Decadent and Depraved," moved to become one of Hunter S. Thompson's most popular works, launching an entire genre known as gonzo journalism.

That said, we are naturally wired in a way that if we have an entire week to finish a project, we will turtle-crawl through it. But if it's due in 3 hours, our focus and productivity will instantly shoot through the roof.

Do things early and ahead of time - so we've been told time and time again. Still, books and pages of history are dominated by stories of famous procrastinators.

Let me provoke you the more. I believe you know the famous Architect Frank Lloyd Wright? Do you know that he designed the most esteemed masterpiece, Fallingwater, in just two hours, spurred on by the fact that his client was about to visit to check on his progress?

Also, Author Margaret Atwood, the Canadian poet, novelist, literary critic, essayist, teacher, environmental activist, and inventor said that she "used to spend the morning procrastinating and worrying, then plunge into the manuscript in a frenzy of anxiety around 3:00."

But all those mentioned above can't beat Herman Melville's procrastination that he reportedly had his wife chain him to his desk so he could finish writing Moby Dick.

Well, now, I know that some of you are reading this and telling yourselves "Correlation doesn't imply causation!" And, fair enough, you're right. But what these stories show is that these people succeeded in big ways, at least despite their procrastination.

This isn't the most enjoyable (or healthy) approach, but you can't deny its effectiveness. It's just the human thing and most times we get the better result this way.

Before we go deeper into this guide I will like us to reflect with an operating definition of the word "procrastination" as debates over whether procrastination is good or bad often arise simply from a difference in semantics.

There are a handful of psychological scientists and procrastination opposers like Timothy A. Pychyl, who in his humble-self defined procrastination as a "voluntary delay of intended action with the expectation of a possible worse outcome."

But this chapter focuses on Merriam-Webster's definition of procrastination. It defines "procrastinate" as "to put off intentionally the doing of something that should be done."

In other words: Procrastination is when you have time to do something, but you deliberately wait until the last minute to do it.

While writing a guide "in praise" of procrastination can be contentious, it's difficult to hold that procrastination does have its upsides.

Schedule something fun (or expensive):

This technique combines the power of deadlines with the anticipation of a reward.

Life is overwhelming sometimes. This moment you're thinking of how to create a post for your blog site, the next moment you're thinking of how to post on an employer's social media page.

There are also kids, your partner, home, and other hobbies or interest you might have. The weeks already seem packed to you as a work from home mum or Dad before they even started.

One way to incorporate self-care into your weekly routine is scheduling fun. In fact, according to psychologytoday, "30% of the happiness you get from a given experience comes from anticipating it."

In other words: You can suck 30% more happiness from the fun stuff you're already doing just by putting it on your calendar.

When you scribble a reminder into your planner, you'll see it every day. You'll get a little jolt of joy thinking about how much fun you're going to have at that dinner party, concert, beach day, or camping trip. This idea helps reposition your mental state to work.

In summary: Want to finish your work by 4 pm today? Simple. Just schedule a fun activity for 2:30 pm.

Bonus points if the activity is:

- Expensive
- Paid in advance
- Non-refundable
- Something you do with a group of friends

It sure would be jaw-gnashing to lose money, miss out on fun, and let down your friends. So, it's time to put the pedal to the metal!

CHAPTER 2

ADD VIRTUAL SOCIAL PRESSURE

E ver noticed at the gym how you move faster, exercise harder, and restless when other people are watching you?

The same goes for working at home. If you want to max out your productivity, add in some social accountability.

This could be as simple as telling people you're going to finish something by a certain time and asking them to check in with you.

To crank things up a notch, I most times Livestream my writing sessions on Facebook with friends to help me stay on task.

Knowing someone else could be watching your computer screen at any given moment pressures you to stay on task (and stay off fun-spun communities on Reddit).

Use (extreme) rewards and punishments:

My hardworking good friend, I'm not talking about treating yourself to an ice cream cone if you finish your work (although that could work).

I'm talking about taking things to the EXTREME. Things that will glue you into completing the task you've started already.

Things like these:

- o I can't eat until I get this done.
- o I can't talk until I get this done.
- o I can't sleep until I get this done.
- o I can't stand up until I get this done.
- o I can't go to the bathroom until I get this done.

When you're hungry or your bladder is about to explode, you'll finish work at hyperspeed. It works perfectly for me and so many other lazy asses like you.

Plan a fun work night (perhaps with alcohol if you're of age):

So far all our remote work productivity hacks involve some sort of pressure. Yeah, that's because we tend to accomplish more when we are under a threat.

But also, too much pressure can be overwhelming and actually have an ANTI-productive effect. The moment I start anticipating in my work, I know it's time to take a chill pill and have some fun.

Instead of squeezing out every ounce of productivity and forcing myself to work as fast as possible, I do the OPPOSITE.

I snuggle on the couch, turn on some country music, crack open a beer, and take my sweet time. No worries. No pressure. No rush.

After I get a couple of beers in me, that dreaded project suddenly seems fun! (BTW, if you're a writer like I am, altering your mental state is a great way to overcome writer's block too). You might not finish at record speed, but at least you'll finish.

Drink caffeine strategically:

Speaking of altered mental states, coffee can be the ultimate work from home productivity tool if you know how to use it properly.

Many people like to drink every day. These "many people" want to get desensitized to caffeine, and lose the energizing effect.

Don't do this!

Yeah, I know that most people start drinking caffeine because it makes them feel more alert and improves their mood.

Maybe they have read the psychological effect of this. However, many studies suggest that caffeine actually improves cognitive task performance (memory, attention span, etc.) in the short-term, no doubt.

But unfortunately, these studies fail to consider the participants' caffeine habits. New research from Johns Hopkins Medical School shows that performance increases due to caffeine intake are the result of caffeine drinkers experiencing a short-term reversal of caffeine withdrawal.

By controlling for caffeine use in study participants, John Hopkins researchers found that caffeine-related performance improvement is nonexistent without caffeine withdrawal.

In essence, coming off caffeine reduces your cognitive performance and harms your mood.

The only way to get back to normal is to drink caffeine, and when you do drink it, you feel like it's taking you to new heights. In reality, that caffeine is dragging your performance back to normal for a short period.

I would advise: Instead of drinking coffee just because "that's what people do in the morning", start thinking about it strategically.

Don't waste the energy garnered on mindless activities on admin tasks or reading email.

Instead, save it for important tasks requiring an extra oomph of focus and creativity—like important writing sessions, presentations, client calls, etc.

Lastly, keep your weekends caffeine-free to help reset your tolerance. When you do this, you get a HUGE difference in how potent the productivity buzz is.

.

CHAPTER 3

KILL DISTRACTIONS (USING BROWSER EXTENSIONS)

When you work in the company's office, the bosses and colleagues stay close to ensure you stay on task. Isn't it?

When working at home alone, there's no accountability, nobody watching over your shoulder, and nothing to protect you from getting sucked into the social media vortex.

I can't tell you how many times I've opened YouTube to watch a quick video for work and before I know it an hour has passed and I'm watching crocodile vs. hippo fights.

Or if you're a Redditor who can't take your eyes off some fun comments when it drops on your phone. You say to yourself: let me just give a reply to this then continue work, before you know it, time is gone.

Luckily, if you're prone to falling into this social media temptation, here are some handy Chrome extensions:

Focus 45: Chrome extension that blocks distracting sites for 45-minute intervals.

Try News Feed Eradicator: This extension blocks Facebook newsfeed, allowing you to check Facebook for work without getting sucked in.

Use DF Tube: It works perfectly for those who can't take their eyes off YouTube while working. This extension hides YouTube video recommendations in the sidebar and disables autoplay.

I hope this helps!

Write nightly "old school" to-do lists:

People make two big mistakes when using To-Do Lists:

a. They overcomplicate things.
b. They don't plan.

Both of these can be solved with the "Old School To-Do Method". Grab a pen and notebook and write out the 2-4 tasks you want to accomplish the following day.

o No need to plan out the entire month.
o No need to enter it into a fancy app.
o No need to set a bazillion alarms.
o Just a pen, paper, and quick bullet list.

The trick is doing this BEFORE going to bed. With this practice, you wake up knowing exactly where to start and won't waste half your day planning out your day.

Harness "Aha" moments (you only get 1-3 per day):

Sometimes inspiration strikes at the weirdest times. But when it happens—whether you're showering, folding laundry, watching Netflix, etc—stop what you're doing and take advantage of it!

Working at home gives you flexibility. So if you're zombie-crawling through a project at noon, take a break. Don't fight against the wind.

And when an "Aha" moment jolts you with energy at 10 pm, crack open your laptop and enjoy the wind at your back.

WARNING: This doesn't mean sit around and do nothing until you feel inspired.

Personalize your workspace:

You've probably heard that an organized workspace is a productive workspace. I call bullshit. Although everyone is different.

Some work better at a squeaky clean desk, others thrive in clutter. Some work better in boring empty spaces, others need a stimulating environment. Some work better in silence, others need music.

You have to figure out what works best for YOU. The only requirement is that you're COMFORTABLE.

This might mean having an adjustable desk, perfect ergonomics, and regular stretch breaks. Or it could be propping yourself up in bed with a million pillows (like my girlfriend).

You see that there's no one-size-fits-all. Sample different setups, and carefully choose what works best for you, and screw what everyone else says.

Invest in proper lighting:

If your work involves regular video calls, this one's a no-brainer. Not only does investing in lighting make you look more professional on calls, but it also saves time.

With the aid of one-touch lighting, it won't be necessary to adjust windows, shift desks, and "set up the whole office" before each call. Just flip the switch and you're ready to roll.

And the productivity benefits don't end there. Looking professional on camera boosts your confidence, which in turn sharpens performance. As the saying goes. Look good. Feel good. Play well.

Get PISSED at your work: Who does this task think he is, anyway? Stressing you out. Taking your time. Draining your energy. Screw him!

If you need the motivation to knock out a boring project, make it the enemy. Don't stop working until you destroy it completely.

Sometimes your work has tasks you don't want to do. So don't pretend to love it. Curse at it, hate it, do it out of spite, and then CRUSH IT.

Snoop on your competition (and get jealous):

Work at home productivity is deeply linked with your inner levels of motivation. (And it's hard to stay motivated when you're three steps away from your comfy bed and the next series of Stranger Things loaded on Netflix).

One way to keep your motivation tanked topped up is to spy on your competition.

- o Look at all the work they're doing.
- o Look at all the success they're having.
- o Look at all the money they're making.

And then get jealous. When you realize they're hustling while you're slacking, it'll jolt you back to action.

Stop being a little bitch about it:

You. Have it. GOOD. Everything about you has been enriched with thousands of years of human innovation that takes the drudgery and pain away from a harsh, disease-ridden, back bearing-labor, violence-filled-labor and hardship-filled existence.

Your ancestors would never have imagined life to be this easy. Think about all these if you were born just 200 years ago:

If you had bad eyesight: You better start squinting. There's no cheap solution for that.

If you needed surgery: You better drink some whiskey before a guy saws your body open with a rusty blade while you're still awake.

If you got a weird illness: Some voodoo witch doctor would crush up some random leaves, cut you, rub them in the wound, and hope for the best.

If you wanted to know something: You better hope one of your friends knows. Otherwise, you're out of luck.

If you wanted to travel somewhere: You better be super-duper rich and have 6 months of transit time.

Life then was a complete disaster compared to what we have now!!

Most of you reading this guide have access to what people 100 years ago never dreamt of.

You have access to tools and information.

You're reading via a mobile App that people from 200 years ago couldn't even fathom would exist. Yet here you are complaining that "you don't know what to write."

Understand that your work will never be 100% perfect. So just type something out then go back and edit it. It's the best way to just start.

Have it in mind that it's not the end of the world if you write something crappy. Just edit or delete it later. So quit being a little bitter ass and finish off your work.

Just don't do it:

"Just don't do it? You mean, like, let it sit there unfinished forever?"

If a task has been on your to-do list for 2-3 days and you keep pushing it back, it clearly ain't that important, is it?

Turns out, only a very small percentage of tasks are TRULY essential. Sometimes working from home productivity simply means knowing what NOT to do, so you have more time for the important stuff.

CHAPTER 4

DON'T ADD STUFF FOR THE TO-DO LIST

THE SAME DAY

Make a to-do list the night before. And once done with that to-do list, no more work is allowed. Never make the mistake of trying to add stuff to the to-do list the same day.

Even if someone so close asks you for something, reply with "Ok I've got it on my calendar for tomorrow!"

Over the years I've done work for different sized companies, companies of my own, different roles, etc.

While I love doing work, sometimes I would keep adding stuff to my to-do lists and IT NEVER ENDED.

5 years back, I remember switching from place to place thinking of some hard rules I must follow so I can maintain a steady amount of work output without facing any sort of burnout. And thankfully, I did.

Since then, I have found making a to-do list BEFORE YOU GO TO BED to be the best way to stay productive during the day.

Making my to-do lists the night before mentally prepares me for what I need to do and allows me to plan the day ahead of time.

Before I draft to-do lists the night before, I'd wake up, go over the work I need to do, write out a ton of tasks, then dread doing them, or maybe not even have enough time in the day because I didn't plan correctly.

Preparing your work the night before is so incredibly important because you can define what a "successful" day of work is.

Once you finish those tasks, your day has been "successful!" You feel achieved and more comfortable to continue with another project on fresh thought.

Never make the mistake of adding stuff to the to-do list the same day. If you keep adding stuff to your to-do list, you will start creating a never-ending to-do list, and you will never be "satisfied" with a good day's work.

If someone asks you for something, reply with "Ok I've got it on my calendar for tomorrow!"

Here are several ways you can politely tell people:

"Ok, I've got it on my calendar for tomorrow!"

"I'll get it to you within 48 hours."

"Got it, it's on my to-do list for tomorrow."

"Awesome, I'll be handling it by 3pm tomorrow."

"I'll get it to you in 24-48 hours."

So when someone asks you for something, assuming it's not 100% urgent, reply with "Ok I've got it on my calendar for tomorrow!"

I'm cruel with my time and energy, so if someone wants a task done, I always tell them I have it on the to-do list for tomorrow.

Some people are not in a position where they can deflect every task for 24 hours, so for these people, they should make it clear which tasks are REQUIRED for the same day, and which are not.

Many times people will promise something right away, which sets the expectation it will be done right away.

For example:

Boss: "Can you make this report?"

You: "Ok I'll do it right away."

But what if you just try to mention you'll do something tomorrow:

GOOD

Boss: "Can you make this report?"

You: "Sure, I'll have it for you by 3pm tomorrow"

If the boss absolutely needs this report earlier, they will mention it.

This exchange wasn't bad at all, and everyone knows the report will be done by 3pm tomorrow. By simply changing the wording of the response, everyone is happy.

CHAPTER 5

WHERE SHOULD YOU STAY WHILE WORKING FROM HOME?

A fan chatted me before the Christmas Eve of 2020 and said, Dan:

"This year I have been working from home due to Covid-19 crisis, my parents are retired. They are in all day banging around. The neighbors are out banging around all day going to the bins putting a few bean cans in the bin, slamming the front door very loudly.

"Even with earplugs it's still very loud and the earplugs get uncomfortable after a while. I love affiliate marketing but since working from home my stress levels are through the roof and my profits are down.

"I work self-employed on affiliate marketing projects. I feel I could get an office but the ones near me are $311 a month and as I'm a fairly small business this is a huge chunk of money to spend.

"Does anyone else you know work at home and have trouble staying focused? Do they maybe rent offices for a day, how do you think people manage this, please? Any help you can give I would be thankful for. Have a nice Christmas boy, I really want to change things in 2021."

I would've advised him to get a space in a reasonably quiet area but he's nagging about the budget already.

I have been working from home for over 9years and before I got a space of my own, I used to live in my parent's home with no doors for 3years working.

For all those nasty times, noise-canceling headphones helped me but it looks like not everyone is satisfied with that today.

There are lots of options to steal from. There are tons of libraries, coffee shops, universities with free WIFI nowadays, and I don't know if your area is that bad not to have these facilities in this year and time.

Even any deserted corner or park in your town could work sharing the 3G connection from your phone. Go quiet places with your fully charged laptop/tablet, or, where there are power slots to plug in your charger. Two hours of quiet in a public library may do wonders.

Wake up really early to get started on your work earlier. Or go to bed later, much later than anyone so you get plenty of breathing space. Whichever suits you better?

However, if the only way you can stay focus is by getting a space then it's cool also. I have my own studio in Chicago and with headphones, I can really focus. I have no business attending to anybody (at home, at least).

Also, I would advise you to really engage yourself with what you're doing. Sometimes, we tend to find distractions because we want to.

Remember we don't even know what the next issue will be even after you get your own place. The point is always to stay focused and don't sweat the small stuff.

CHAPTER 6

How to stay motivated while

working from home

I was with a good friend of mine last year (Denis). He laid complain that birthed this book. His exact words:

"I have started working at home, due to the pandemic we have ongoing. I have a good schedule with regular 20-minute breaks. I use light music to stay motivated while working and I drink water regularly throughout the day.

"However a lot of the week, starting the evening before, I get lazy and the next day I am unproductive. I start work late and go on Reddit and generally being unproductive.

"Please I know you might have some rituals or anything at all I can use to boost my motivation and production levels. Anything to set me in a better mind and to just push forward every day. I know you have gone through this challenge and overcome it. I would be grateful to hear from you." He concluded.

To some of you reading this piece, I know you often feel drained when drafting a piece of writing. Or you can't go past a page while entering the accounting details on the company's QuickBook as the head of Account.

As a content writer for 10 years, I can feel you. Writing is a very manual job. One character at a time, building a word. One word at a time, building sentences.

Then comes paragraphs, followed by a page full of the 3,000-word article on a stretch sometimes. Your knuckles are weak, and your back aching.

Truly, the mountain size work can get demotivating and intimidating at times and that's why I will be discussing some ways you can supercharge your writing motivations.

However, this strategy below isn't for freelance writers only, it encompasses all industries for everyone who needs the motivation to thrive in working from home amidst the various agents of distraction in our homes.

Let's kickstart:

Watch Motivational Videos on YouTube

If you think motivational videos are cliché, I will not convince you otherwise. Many people perceive motivational talkers as marketers who just want to sell. Hence, they don't want to feel like they're just fuel for their marketing machine.

People who do this, for me, are putting discipline above motivation, and there's nothing wrong with that too, as discipline is inevitable.

But here's my take – motivational videos are effective to give you hope. I listen to it when I'm down because I usually find solace in them.

Those minutes of talks can pump you up and make you work for hours on end. Even though the effect may last only a few hours, why not use that boost every single day? It's only for the better, right?

How long will I continue to listen to motivational videos?

Well, it depends on you. Personally, I don't do that all day; I only go to YouTube to listen to such videos when my head is heavy. Or when I'm stuck at work and needed some ginger to keep powering me on.

So you need to play smart on your own as the same motivational video won't be as effective on the 2nd, 3rd, or 4th day. Keep introducing newness to your brain. Luckily, there are hundreds of videos available to seamlessly switch from on YouTube, today.

You can pick a group of people to listen to. My first choice is Gary Vaynerchuk. Seriously – this guy is breathing fire. David Goggins can help too. Just pick a few, and make sure to change it up from time to time.

This is just one of the learning curve you should follow to continue pushing yourself into a discipline in all endeavors. But building that discipline is the hardest part.

But if you're able to master discipline, even on days you don't feel motivated to work, days you feel overhauled and totally empty, your discipline will take over and get the job done.

Read Pages of a Book

As a writer, you are as good as what you've read. As a computer engineer, you can't rely completely on your own instinct to do things.

Some people are better informed, who have garnered more experience in the same field as you that you need to steal some ideas from. Reading has helped me a lot with my motivation as a freelance blogger (side job).

I don't know your area of specialization, but whatever it is, you need to read books from other experts. You can start with 2-5 pages if you are not a habitual reader and wrap it off in a week.

More so, it's not must you finish a book. Read up the part you think is enough to refresh your mind, and gives you thousands of reasons to avoid procrastination, then you're well on your way.

Besides the educative part of reading is that it will help you replace 'low state thoughts' with positive powerful perspectives.

What's more, reading helps supercharge your brain with words. It has a way of getting your creative juices flowing too.

I tend to read philosophy, psychology, self-help, and motivational books. Choose a niche for yourself depending on what inspires you.

I included motivational because I've seen motivational content helps a lot to get moving. I mean - how can I not get pumped by reading how Lionel Messi started from the bottom and made it to the mountain peak?

That said, don't just limit yourself to books. Pick some articles you like and read too. As long as they are informative, you're well on your way. But stay away from humor because it relaxes you, and promotes lethargic behavior.

Note: your reads don't have to be rocket science manuals. Carefully run through the subjects then pick the one that lifts your spirit and dig right in.

Watch a Documentary

If you prefer watching over reading, documentaries are for you. Whenever I don't feel like reading or going on YouTube, I pick up the TV remote and select Nat Geo World. I love animal documentaries.

You can watch any program you feel has some help to your person. Be it anything as long as you are consuming quality content that refreshes your mind, you're set.

I picked documentaries because hearing voices of people speak of past events and some earthly wonders triggers my brain to get engage and active.

This I believe explains why we're more aware in groups, and mind wanderers when alone. In other words, documentaries stir your brain out of laziness. Thus, making writing much easier for you.

However, you'll want to keep your selections 10 to 15 minutes long. Else, you'll end up dropping a lot of mental energy, which again can haul you back to the uninspired state.

For documentary sources, I prefer you to start with Bloomberg and National Geography. But I wouldn't want to choose for you as that will seem like stopping you from something you find interesting, just because I didn't prefer the channel.

And a caution - don't consider hourly news to be knowledge here. Imagine headlines like Iraq about to Invade the White House, Russia planning on attacking its non-allies, and so on.

That's why you should leave daily news out of it. News is temporary information and can spike your stress. I want you to stick to solid evergreen information.

Meditate to Sort out Your Ruffled Mind

Yes, you just heard that right. You need to shave your head and become a monk in the freezing temperatures of the peaks of the Himalayas. For inspiration. To work.

Okay, that was a bad joke. And if you agree my jokes are bad, I won't tell you otherwise. Maybe I will watch some more Bill Burr comedy and memorize some sentences. Anyway, the fact remains that meditating can help you sort out your ruffled mind.

I've meditated in the past and can tell it is amazing to attain mental clarity and cognitive control of your mind.

While not my favorite or most effective strategy for eradicating procrastination, scientific studies show it helps with motivation levels.

One way or the other, procrastination has a lot to do with clarity. Once you have the exact steps you need to walk, you can start to walk that path.

I've always done guided meditation. And they seem to be in full swing nowadays. If you want to try them out, you can find them on SoundCloud.

Listen To Podcasts

Podcasts also help you engage your brain and fight procrastination. If you're the type that slouches before a writing session, why you dive into a 15-minute podcast to get your brain pumping?

You can pick any topic of your choice - psychology, motivational, entrepreneurship, mindset - are to name a few.

I have my favorite motivators in The GaryVee Audio Experience and Joe Rogan Experience. These guys are maestros because they've been in this for a long time, and as such, you'll never run out of quality things to hear.

And since you can play them in the background when working, it makes them a breeze to carry anywhere.

Once the podcast is finished, jump straight to work. The momentum of your brain will shift from engaging to create.

Exercise To Awaken Your Endorphins

You can choose to walk, jog, or lift weights - anything you find suitable. The point is - you need to challenge your body physically.

Any type of physical exercise introduces discipline to your body and releases the endorphins in your brain, which help you slash down stress, and skyrocket happiness. That way, you will be able to approach writing with a clear mind.

Another thing, our bodies are not designed/created to be in the same place for hours on end. It craves movement.

Personally, I run from one end to another of my apartment for 10 - 20 minutes. Sometimes I also do some wall push-ups (can't pull off the ground ones, YES, I'm fat).

I also stroll from one end of the house to another. The most important thing here is that - you need to activate your physical and mental energy through physical exertion.

Once done, jump on your computer and start writing. You will feel some unique sense of aliveness.

And Lastly, Start Now

With all that said, if you don't apply the techniques, then we've both wasted our time. Pick one move, apply it and see how it eliminates the lethargic, uninspired you. One brick at a time.

CONCLUSION

S ome scholars have argued that we are exactly moving in the direction the elite wants people to go:

"Stay at home where 85% of citizens will be unemployed till 2030. Own nothing anymore as everything will be business to subscription.

"Receive basic income. Spend it on food and digital goods. Centralize economy so only big cooperation will stay which are under full control.

"Eliminate all small and mid-size businesses etc.

Remember you decide with your money which route you are going to support.

"And that the cooperation route is a full dominance route which Hitler or Stalin could only dream about."

"They said 10 years ago that their goal is that 4 families will share a car. Since a car is only used by 5% and the rest of the time it stays. It will be an autonomous car called via an app.

"At that time we thought how it would be possible that people would give up their personal car and the only logical explanation was that they won't be able to afford to buy a new car (B2S remember?).

Supporting cooperation instead of the small and mid-size company will lead that you will be fully dependable on grants from the government.

Take your time to think about it again and again if the luxury of laziness is worth your financial freedom because with industry4.0 majority will have no other income."

Well, I don't poke my nose into propaganda as this huge. But all I have to say is that work from home is here to stay for long and you have to adapt no matter what. Unless the government's relief fund is enough to cover your family up, then you can be lazy.

Are you aware that Twitter CEO 'Jack Dorsey' allows 'forever' work from home? I bet you don't.

Understanding this option is not suitable for everyone, Dorsey is keeping the door open for those who wish to work within the traditional office structure. He's leaving the decision to either work from home or at the office in the hands of his employees.

You wouldn't want to risk your life to the office all because you feel lazy while working from home? Why not build on any of the strategies explained here to get yourself active and always motivated?

If Jack could say that, don't you think he sees the potential after he witnessed the first two months and probably has the vision and knows a thing or two than the rest of us?

The ball is in your court to do whatever with it. You've been offered the flexibility you once wished for to work at your own convenient time and now you have it.

Do you still want to continue nagging and wailing about your neighbors, kids, and other frivolities?

The choice is yours!

ABOUT THE AUTHOR

Daniel Welsh is a life coach. He is a mentor, teacher, a well-drilled, skillful, and knowledgeable person with specialized tools and techniques to assists you in looking at a bigger and holistic picture and then collaborate with you in exploring specific solutions for your life.

He is also an accomplished and result-oriented professional with 10 years of excellent experience propelling digital marketing campaigns to achieve or outperform sales targets.

(Optional)

Made in United States
Troutdale, OR
07/11/2023

11130754R00029